WWF
WORLD
WIDE
FUND
FOR NATURE

By Kirsty Holmes

WORLD
CHARITIES

©2018
BookLife Publishing
King's Lynn
Norfolk PE30 4LS

All rights reserved.
Printed in Malaysia.

A catalogue record for this book is available from the British Library.

ISBN: 978-1-78637-315-1

Written by:
Kirsty Holmes

Edited by:
Holly Duhig

Designed by:
Dan Scase

Words that look like **THIS** are explained in the glossary on page 31.

CHARITY & GIVING

Some people give money to charity.

WHAT IS 'CHARITY'?

Every person and animal on planet Earth is part of a GLOBAL COMMUNITY. We all need similar things to survive and grow. Every person needs food to eat, fresh water to drink and somewhere safe to live. But, even though we all need the same things, we don't all have the same things. Some people and animals have access to more RESOURCES or are better protected from danger than others.

DONATION

Some people help animals in danger, like these orangutans.

For example, in some countries there may not be enough food for people to eat, or there may be wars or natural disasters which have taken away people's homes. Animals are also in danger all over the world, often because of human activity.

Many people see these problems and feel a strong need to make it better. They help by giving time, money or other resources, such as food, to those in need. This type of giving is called charity.

Some people give their time to help others.

WHAT IS A CHARITY?

When a group of people get together and form an organisation to help people, animals or other good causes, we call that organisation a charity. Charities can be huge, INTERNATIONAL organisations with thousands of people working for them, or they can be small groups working for a local good cause. People donate their time and money to charities, and in turn, the charities organise these resources to help people in the best way possible.

Some charities are like big companies, organising thousands of people and millions of pounds.

St Peter's Hospice Shop
For Patients, Families and Bristol

People can do silly things to raise money for charity!

Small local charities, like hospices or animal sanctuaries, rely on people's donations.

KEY WORDS ABOUT CHARITIES

- **Donation** a gift of time, money or goods to a charity
- **Donor** a person or company who makes a donation
- **Volunteer** a person who works for a charity but isn't paid
- **Fundraising** collecting money for a charity
- **Awareness** making sure people know about a charity or issue
- **Campaign** work in an organised way towards a goal
- **Activist** person who campaigns and raises awareness on a topic

5

THE WORLD WIDE FUND FOR NATURE

THE WWF MISSION STATEMENT

"WWF is the world's leading independent **CONSERVATION** organisation.

Our mission is to create a world where people and wildlife can **THRIVE** together.

To achieve our mission, we're finding ways to help transform the future for the world's wildlife, rivers, forests and seas; pushing for a reduction in **CARBON EMISSIONS** that will avoid catastrophic climate change; and pressing for measures to help people **LIVE SUSTAINABLY**, within the means of our one planet.

We're acting now to make this happen."

Find out more about the WWF's mission at
https://www.wwf.org.uk/who-we-are

A mission statement tells you what a charity stands for, who they want to help, and why.

PROTECTING **YOUR** PLANET

The World Wide Fund for Nature – known as the WWF – is a charity and organisation working to protect wildlife across the planet. They work to look after the wilderness, and protect the Earth's natural environment from damage or destruction by humans.

The WWF logo is a panda, based on a real panda called Chi Chi. It was thought she would make a good logo as she was cute, with large eyes!

The WWF Office in Japan

HOW THE WWF BEGAN

The WWF was started in 1961, in Switzerland. A group of people who were interested in protecting wildlife noticed that, although there were many people with the skills needed to do this, they did not have the money or organisation needed to make a real difference. The WWF was formed to provide an organisation who could collect money, guide people and support wildlife conservation around the world. It grew over the years to become one of the biggest animal conservation charities in the world.

Prince Philip, from the UK, was one of the first **patrons** of the WWF.

WHAT DO THE WWF DO?

At the moment, most of the work done by the WWF is focused on conserving three BIOMES: oceans and coasts, forests, and freshwater systems. They also work to conserve habitats of priority species such as tigers, polar bears, orangutans and marine turtles. There are currently 17 priority species.

SNOW LEOPARD

MOUNTAIN GORILLA

ADÉLIE PENGUIN

PRIORITY SPECIES

- ADÉLIE PENGUINS
- AFRICAN ELEPHANTS
- AFRICAN LIONS
- AFRICAN RHINOS
- AMUR LEOPARDS

- ASIAN ELEPHANTS
- ASIAN RHINOS
- DOLPHINS
- GIANT PANDAS
- JAGUARS

- MARINE TURTLES
- MOUNTAIN GORILLAS
- ORANGUTANS
- POLAR BEARS
- SNOW LEOPARDS

- TIGERS
- YANGTZE FINLESS PORPOISES

The WWF works to raise awareness and educate people, teaching us to value nature and the natural world around us. They also promote SUSTAINABLE living, which means living in a way that doesn't use up the planet's natural resources without replacing them. People who work for the WWF also help with conservation efforts to protect wildlife and the habitats they live in. They do this through campaigning, raising money, and supporting people to look after the wildlife in their areas.

The WWF's president is His Royal Highness Prince Charles. Prince Charles became president of the WWF in 2001, the 50th Anniversary of the charity. Adding such an important voice to the work of the WWF has helped the charity raise awareness. The Prince has made speeches talking about the WWF's work, worked with businesses, and visited schools, challenging and inspiring people to think about the natural world and the environment.

Prince Charles

WWF FACT FILE

- **Charity Name:** The World Wide Fund for Nature
- **Also Known As:** The WWF, The World Wildlife Fund
- **Started:** 29th April 1961
- **Staff:** Over 6,200
- **Supporters:** Over 5 Million
- **Money Raised:** Over $11.5 Billion US Dollars
- **Main Areas:** Wildlife Conservation, Climate Change, Sustainable Living
- **Fundraising:** Donations, Business Sponsorship, Adoptions & LEGACIES

Find out more at
www.gowild.wwf.org.uk

NATURE IN DANGER

CLIMATE CHANGE

One of the biggest threats to wildlife, humans and habitats is climate change. The climate is the usual weather we would expect to see in a place. Around the world, the climate of many places is changing dramatically. The overall temperature of the Earth is getting warmer through a process called global warming and this is causing the ice at the Earth's polar regions to melt. This, in turn, is causing the sea levels to rise. Climate change is affecting lots of species of wildlife, as they lose their habitats, or can't cope with the changing weather.

ADÉLIE PENGUINS & POLAR BEARS

Adélie penguins live in the Antarctic in the south, and polar bears live in the Arctic in the north. Both species are losing the sea ice they need to live on. Adélie penguins are losing their main food, krill, which BREED under the ice. Polar bears are losing their own food too: seals, who also need the sea ice to breed.

KRILL

ADÉLIE PENGUIN

Adélie penguins are very good swimmers.

POLAR BEAR

SUSTAINABLE LIVING & TRADE

Humans live in all areas of the planet, and we use almost all the natural resources available to us. This can be bad for nature, however, as we often destroy land, habitats or the wildlife itself in the process.

Large areas of forest are cut down every year so people can use the land. This destroys important habitats and adds to global warming, as the trees can no longer remove **CARBON DIOXIDE** from the air.

Pollution comes from transport, factories and **URBAN DEVELOPMENT**, as well as large-scale farming. We are damaging the air, soil and water that we all need to live.

Humans like to eat fish and seafood, but if we catch too many fish, it affects the balance of life in the oceans. Large fishing **TRAWLERS** also catch other species like dolphins and turtles in their nets.

HUMAN-WILDLIFE CONFLICT

Humans and animals all share the same planet. But sometimes, humans and animals who live very closely can come into CONFLICT over resources such as food, land or safety. There are over seven billion people living on the planet and, as there are more and more of us, we need more and more space. When humans move into animal territory, the people and the animals can clash, putting the safety of both at risk. Animals can eat people's crops, trample their property, or even attack the people themselves. People, in return, can trap, poison or kill the animals.

Baboons in Namibia can kill livestock, such as goats or sheep.

POLAR BEARS VS PEOPLE

As polar bears lose their ice habitats and sources of food, they are driven ever-closer to human SETTLEMENTS. Their amazing sense of smell attracts them towards villages to look for food. Polar bears are powerful predators, and have been known to attack humans – more than 20 direct attacks on people around these towns have been recorded. People trap and shoot polar bears to prevent these attacks.

Polar bears approach human settlements looking for food.

Many of the natural resources humans use, like wood for building, are traded legally, sustainably and safely. However, illegal or unsustainable trading in animals and their body parts can be very dangerous and some species are being pushed to the brink of EXTINCTION. Animals in danger from this include elephants, who are killed by POACHERS for their tusks, and tigers who are killed for their fur, skins and for use in TRADITIONAL MEDICINES.

IVORY BROOCH

Illegal hunting and poaching are almost as dangerous to species as habitat destruction.

ELEPHANT TUSKS

Elephant tusks are made of ivory, which is worth a lot of money. Around 20,000 elephants each year are killed for their tusks.

Turtles, like this hawksbill sea turtle, are hunted for their meat and shells, and in some cultures, their eggs too.

Rhinos are poached for their horns, which are used in traditional medicines.

Snow leopards are hunted for their beautiful, thick fur.

DO IT FOR YOUR PLANET

The WWF are working in lots of areas around the world to protect wildlife and help people to live in harmony with nature.

TIME

One of the most important resources a charity can have is people giving their time. From volunteers working for free to paid, full-time EMPLOYEES and celebrity ambassadors, time given to helping animals and nature is vitally important to their work.

VOLUNTEERS

Many people give their time to charities for free, doing things such as collecting clothing and items to sell in the charity shops, or collecting change for donations. Other people might work in a local charity shop or collect money through fundraising. These people are called volunteers.

The WWF also has a Youth Volunteer Program. Young people aged between 19 and 27 can give their time for free, and travel and work alongside the WWF around the world, either educating people, or out in the wild helping animals.

Volunteers work in charity shops for free, raising money to support the charity.

WWF volunteers go to show support when people run **MARATHONS** to raise money. This is called Team Panda and anyone can sign up to cheer! Find out more on page 30.

WWF

Home

Everyone who works for the WWF has an important part to play in keeping the charity running.

WORKING FOR THE WWF

Many people are so passionate about nature and wildlife that they make it their **CAREER**. Charities are huge organisations, so there are many opportunities to do something good for a living.

WWF UK employs around 350 people at their headquarters in Surrey, called the Living Planet Centre. Some people work in other countries, working directly with projects – these people can be environmental scientists, engineers or project managers.

Others work to raise money, provide publicity, and manage the day-to-day running of a huge organisation. Charities couldn't exist without people working for them!

DO IT FOR YOUR PLANET

MONEY

Charities need money to be able to do their work. But where do they get it from?

DONATIONS

People give money to the WWF as gifts. This can be small amounts, like loose change given to collection pots, or huge donations of up to millions of pounds. Some people set up a regular payment from their bank account to the WWF and give a small amount every month. Other people make one-off donations, perhaps from a fundraising activity. Even small amounts can add up quickly.

ADOPTIONS

Some people support the WWF by 'adopting' an animal. You choose an animal species to support and then pay a small amount of money every month. The money goes towards the charity, and they use it to support your chosen species. In return, you get regular updates and letters about your animal – and you might even get a cuddly one to keep!

Many people give adoptions as gifts – would you like to adopt an animal for your birthday? There are lots to choose from. Find out more at https://support.wwf.org.uk/adopt-an-animal/

FUNDRAISING

The WWF relies on people raising money to support the charity's work with animals. People can raise money in lots of ways – by asking lots of people to give just a little, or asking one or two people or big businesses to give a lot!

Fundraising is often done by volunteers.

Tennis star Andy Murray has been working with the WWF to promote and protect tigers in the wild.

Popstar Ellie Goulding has been working with the WWF to promote Earth Hour. Find out more on page 25.

CELEBRITY AMBASSADORS

Many famous people find they can speak to lots of people because they have a lot of fans and followers on social media. Celebrities working with the WWF use this opportunity to speak out for animals and wildlife and talk about the WWF.

BUSINESSES & SPONSORS

These are just some of the brands that support the WWF.

Big businesses work with the WWF by donating money, working to raise awareness, or changing the way they work to help animals and wildlife.

Find out more about how YOU can raise funds for the WWF on page 28.

COCA-COLA

JOHN WEST

MARKS & SPENCER

ALPRO

17

DO IT FOR YOUR PLANET

AWARENESS

By raising awareness and telling people about the problems in the world of wildlife, the WWF can inspire people to help or get involved.

SOCIAL MEDIA

Social media is a very powerful tool in raising awareness. The WWF uses social media to raise awareness, share stories and successes, and let people know about nature and their work to protect it. Ask an adult with an account on one of these sites to show you the WWF's work, and talk with you about what you see there.

@wwf_uk

@wwfunitedkingdom

@wwf_uk

wwfunitedkingdom

wwfuk

THE WWF AND SKY

The TV service, Sky, have worked with the WWF on the Sky Rainforest Rescue campaign. Together they raised £9.5 million to help protect one billion trees in the Amazon rainforest. This project is still working to protect the rainforests today.

Sky also helped to raise awareness in the UK and Ireland, making eight TV adverts to promote the crucial role of rainforests in preventing climate change, and creating an education programme which allowed 80,000 school children to learn about

rainforests. More than 7.3 million people were made aware of this issue and, as a result, many people did more to help.

Rainforests are essential habitats for many species, like the orangutan.

Find out more about how you can get involved with WWF on page 26.

EDUCATION

The WWF works with schools and teachers to educate and inspire the next generation of nature warriors – that's you! Schools and youth groups such as scouts or youth clubs can find out more about the WWF and sustainable living through the youth programme, or through a visit to the Living Planet Centre. The WWF believe that, by educating children and young people about nature, the planet, and sustainable living, they will **EMPOWER** young people to make good choices, look after our planet, and create a better future.

We can all learn to make better choices and stand up for what we believe in.

SUCCESS STORIES

Through fundraising, education and awareness, and with the help of staff and volunteers, the WWF has done some amazing work for wildlife and nature around the world. Here are some success stories, showing how the charity has made a difference.

SIBERIAN TIGER

TIGERS

HUNTING LAWS HAVE HELPED PROTECT THE TIGERS.

In 2010, the number of tigers in the wild was the lowest it had ever been, with around 3,200 left. This is a drop in numbers of almost 95% since the 20th century began. Tigers were on the brink of extinction.

The WWF worked with local governments in 13 countries where tigers live to agree a special goal: to double the number of tigers to 6,400 by 2022. All 13 countries agreed.

In 2016, for the first time, tiger numbers recovered instead of falling, and grew to 3,900. While still quite a small number, this is an amazing achievement, and it means that the tiger protections are starting to work.

BENGAL TIGER

2022 is the next Chinese Year of the Tiger.

SEA TURTLES

Small communities in coastal areas often rely on fishing for an income, and for food. In Tanzania, a lot of turtles were getting caught up in the nets used by local fishing boats. When this happened, fishermen were not cutting the turtles free, as damaging the nets meant they couldn't use them again and they were afraid to lose their income.

The WWF have set up more than 60 Beach Management Units. The government and community work together, allowing local people to look after and control the beaches. They made rules to limit the amount of fish that boats can catch, and to record when a turtle is seen.

WWF projects in Tanzania, and also in Kenya, have helped the fishermen and the sea life to live together in harmony.

FISHING BOAT AND NETS, TANZANIA

The WWF also buys new fishing nets for any fisherman who damages theirs while cutting a turtle free. This means the local fishermen can help the turtles, and they don't lose their income. Taking care of the beaches and populations of fish also means that the fishermen's incomes are protected, and there are more fish to catch.

THE PARIS CLIMATE AGREEMENT

Ban Ki-Moon, Secretary-General of the **UNITED NATIONS** from 2007 to 2016

On 2nd December, 2015, a record-breaking march took place, with over 785,000 people all over the world getting together in the streets to DEMONSTRATE. The march took place before a very important meeting of the United Nations, known as the COP21. This was a meeting between leaders of 196 countries from all over the world to discuss climate change and global warming, and what should be done.

The WWF marched in London with over 50,000 people and worked with the Climate Coalition to show that the people wanted a fair agreement on climate change. The WWF also worked to influence and inform the governments by writing letters and raising awareness to push for a good deal.

The Eiffel Tower was lit up to celebrate the Paris Climate Agreement.

The COP21 ended with a historic agreement: The Paris Climate Agreement. This agreement was signed by all 196 countries, and they agreed to:

AGREEMENT

- Limit global warming to rising "well below" 2°C
- Reduce greenhouse gas emissions
- Set better and more challenging targets every five years
- Make rich countries help poorer ones by providing "climate finance"

Since the agreement was signed, the WWF have campaigned to pressure countries into staying in the agreement, to stick to their promises, and to set more ambitious targets to reduce climate change.

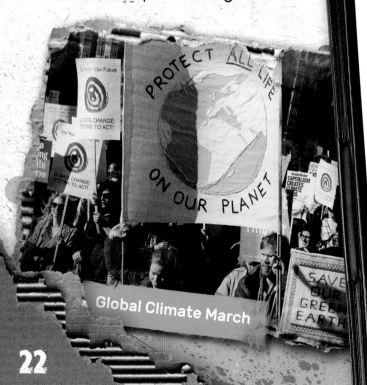

Global Climate March

ELEPHANTS IN THE BACK YARD

Corbett National Park in India has seen conflict between farmers and elephants fall by over 60% in just one year! The WWF's education and training has helped villagers learn how to stop elephants eating their crops. By using solar fences, they can stop elephants trampling their food. They also stop elephants eating all their crops by planting crops to sell that elephants don't like, like mint or chilli. The villagers can then sell the chilli on, and make even more money so there is no need to shoot or harm the elephants anymore.

PROTECTING THE PLANET

These are just a few of the amazing successes achieved by the WWF and their work. They work in hundreds of countries, with thousands of people and millions of pounds to protect our natural world for the future. They co-ordinate people, businesses, governments, WWF members and patrons to create a world where people and nature can live and thrive in harmony.

Artist Paulo Grangeon took 1,600 papier-mâché pandas on a world tour, EXHIBITING them at important locations around the world, to raise awareness for the WWF and the environment.

1,600 pandas were made because there were only 1,600 left at that time in the wild. Today, there are around 1,860 – the WWF's work is making a difference.

GREEN AMBASSADORS

Green Ambassadors is the WWF's exciting new scheme for schools. The aim of the scheme is to inspire and encourage a new generation of sustainability champions. Schools and youth groups can sign up to the scheme, and the WWF will send ideas and resources to help their school start a 'green team' to help pupils – like you – look after your schools' sustainability and CARBON FOOTPRINT. Let's take a look at what it's all about below.

PLANT2PLATE

The Plant2Plate campaign looks at sustainability in our food. Schools can think about how sustainable the food in their canteen is, where it comes from, and even grow their own!

TV Presenter Ben Fogle is a WWF Ambassador, and helped choose the winning schools in 2017.

GREEN AMBASSADOR CHAMPIONS

Registered schools can enter the Green Ambassador Awards. Each year, the WWF looks for the best green school, the best green teacher, and the best green team. In 2017, 12 schools won awards!

COULD YOUR SCHOOL GO GREEN?

Ask your teacher if your school is signed up to the Green Ambassadors scheme. If they aren't, why not start your own Green Team and get signed up! Tell your teacher to go to:
http://wwfschoolsscheme.education.co.uk/
and become a Green Ambassador school today!

Find out more at https://www.wwf.org.uk/get-involved/schools/school-campaigns/plant2plate

Schools that are more sustainable help protect the planet for you when you're grown up, and save money too!

EARTH HOUR

In 2008, WWF Australia came up with an idea to get Australians talking about climate change, and organised an event to get people to switch their lights off for one hour, all at the same time.

This idea grew, and now is a huge event around the world. Hundreds of millions of people switch off their lights, and organise events to show they care about the future of the planet. Major cities now switch off their lights on landmarks, such as the Eiffel Tower, and some websites even join in. The event helps people to think about saving energy and sustainable power, and to talk about climate change.

2018 marks the 10th year since Earth Hour began.

TAKE PART

Discuss Earth Hour at home and see if your family can take part in the next one. Schools can join in too - Earth Hour is at night, but your school can hold their own Earth Hour during the day, and switch off all electricity. Maybe your class could hold an assembly and talk about Earth Hour and why it matters?

Everyone can raise awareness. People can be very powerful when they all come together for an idea.

GET INVOLVED

Maybe what you've found out about the WWF and the planet has inspired you to take action. Let's look at how you can make a difference and support the WWF.

DO!

Could you or your school organise a fundraising event? How can you help local wildlife? Here are some ideas.

SPONSOR ME!

Hold an event, take on a challenge, or do something amazing, and get people to sponsor you. Run, walk, climb, bounce, skip... it's up to you!

SELL, SELL, SELL!

Hold a cake sale – maybe you could make tiger-striped cupcakes or monkey cookies? Make sure you use sustainable ingredients and talk to your customers about the WWF.

Stay safe. Make sure an adult helps you organise your event.

VOLUNTEER

Is there a local group in your hometown that looks after the environment? Could you talk to an adult about starting one? Looking after local wildlife is important too – from bees to field mice, hedgehogs in the garden or molehills in the local park, all nature needs protecting.

DISCUSS!

Become a youth activist and raise awareness in your own communities. Here are some ways to get people talking.

WRITE A LETTER

Is there a local or worldwide nature issue you are passionate about? Write a letter to your school newsletter, your local newspaper, or even to the national press!

START A CONVERSATION

Ask to speak to your class, or even your whole school assembly, about the WWF and their work. Tell them why it matters, what you have read, and how they can help.

Make your talk interesting!

WEAR IT WILD

Wear It Wild is a WWF campaign where you dress as a wild animal for the day, and donate to the WWF. See if you can get your whole school involved! When someone asks you why you've swapped your school uniform for a lion suit, tell them about the WWF and why you're...

DOING IT FOR THE PLANET!

Find out more about Wear It Wild at https://wearitwild.wwf.org.uk/

DONATE!

Money, time or goods – everyone can contribute something.

A MILE OF PENNIES

Could your teacher help you organise a mile of pennies? Chalk out a line that is a mile long in your playground. You might have to curl it up like a snake! Ask people to line up pennies on the line until it's full – then collect them up and donate them!

ADOPT AN ANIMAL

For a birthday present, or as a class project, choose an animal to 'adopt'. Your monthly contribution or one-off payment pays for the WWF to protect that species and you get regular updates and news.

Find out more at https://support.wwf.org.uk/adopt-an-animal/

HELP OTHERS, HELP WWF

Offer to do some chores around the house or at school in return for donations to WWF. Get your siblings or friends involved too!

LOSE YOUR VOICE TO USE YOUR VOICE

Hold a sponsored silence – don't speak for a whole day to stand up for animals who don't have a voice. Get people to sponsor you and donate to the WWF.

Make some signs or leaflets to tell people why you aren't speaking, and why you're supporting the WWF!

SMALL CHANGES, BIG IMPACT

Changing the world starts with changing your world. Little choices we make can make a big difference.

LIVE SUSTAINABLY

Talking to your school or family about living sustainably can have a big impact. Think about how you can:

REDUCE your rubbish and carbon footprint

REUSE things instead of throwing them away

RECYCLE things so we don't need as many natural resources

When you buy products made from wood, paper or palm oil, always make sure they are sustainably sourced. Look for the FSC logo or information on the packaging to tell you if something is sustainable.

JOIN THE WWF

You will need an adult for this one, but the best way to support the WWF is to become a member. For a monthly donation, you will receive a member's pack with activities for you and your family, and other gifts. You will also know you are supporting a charity that is helping to save the planet for you and your future.

THE WWF AND THEIR MISSION:

https://www.wwf.org.uk/who-we-are

TEAM PANDA:

https://www.wwf.org.uk/get-involved/fundraise/volunteer

ADOPT AN ANIMAL:

https://support.wwf.org.uk/adopt-an-animal/

GREEN AMBASSADORS:

https://www.wwf.org.uk/get-involved/schools/green-ambassadors

EARTH HOUR:

https://www.wwf.org.uk/earthhour

Write to your local **MP** to tell them about climate change and show you care: https://www.writetothem.com/

GLOSSARY

BIOMES	A LARGE COMMUNITY OF PLANTS AND ANIMALS WHICH HAVE SOMETHING IN COMMON
BREED	TO PRODUCE OFFSPRING
CARBON DIOXIDE	A NATURAL, COLOURLESS GAS THAT IS FOUND IN THE AIR
CARBON EMISSIONS	THE HARMFUL GASES PRODUCED BY CARS AND OTHER VEHICLES
CARBON FOOTPRINT	HOW MUCH CARBON DIOXIDE IS RELEASED INTO THE ATMOSPHERE BY A PERSON OR THING
CAREER	A JOB OR OCCUPATION WHICH A PERSON HAS FOR A LONG TIME
CONFLICT	ACTIVE DISAGREEMENT
CONSERVATION	WORK THAT IS DONE TO PROTECT SOMETHING FROM DAMAGE OR HARM
DEMONSTRATE	TO JOIN IN AN ACTIVE PROTEST, FOR EXAMPLE A MARCH
EMPLOYEES	PEOPLE WHO WORK FOR A COMPANY OR ORGANISATION
EMPOWER	TO GIVE POWER TO SOMEONE OR SOMETHING, TO MAKE THEM FEEL POWERFUL
EXHIBITING	DISPLAYING A PIECE OF ART FOR PEOPLE TO SEE
EXTINCTION	WHEN THERE ARE NO MORE LIVING MEMBERS OF A CERTAIN SPECIES
GLOBAL COMMUNITY	THE PEOPLE AND NATIONS OF THE WORLD
INTERNATIONAL	BETWEEN MORE THAN ONE NATION
LEGACIES	GIFTS TO A CHARITY LEFT IN A PERSON'S WILL WHEN THEY DIE
LIVE SUSTAINABLY	LIVE IN A WAY THAT DOES LITTLE HARM TO THE PLANET
MARATHONS	A RUNNING RACE WHICH IS 26.3 MILES LONG
PATRONS	PEOPLE WHO GIVE FINANCIAL OR OTHER SUPPORT TO A PERSON, ORGANIZATION, OR CAUSE
POACHERS	PEOPLE WHO HUNT ANIMALS ILLEGALLY
RESOURCES	THINGS THAT ARE USEFUL OR OF VALUE
SETTLEMENTS	PLACES PEOPLE LIVE PERMANENTLY, LIKE VILLAGES OR TOWNS
SUSTAINABLE	ABLE TO BE MAINTAINED AT A CERTAIN RATE OR LEVEL
THRIVE	GROW OR DEVELOP WELL
TRADITIONAL MEDICINES	MEDICINES WHICH HAVE DEVELOPED OVER TIME IN CERTAIN COMMUNITIES
TRAWLERS	A FISHING BOAT THAT PULLS A LARGE, CONE-SHAPED NET THROUGH THE SEA TO CATCH FISH
UNITED NATIONS	AN INTERNATIONAL PEACE ORGANISATION
URBAN DEVELOPMENT	CLEARING LAND SO THAT TOWNS OR CITIES CAN BE BUILT

INDEX

Photo Credits

Front Cover – Fernan Archilla. 2 – Fernan Archilla. 4 – tristan tan, Aysezgicmeli, Dmytro Zinkevych. 5 – Rawpixel.com, LandFox, Jacek Wojnarowski. 6 Volodymyr Burdiak, Eric Isselee, Dmitry Laudin, Sergey Uryadnikov, timsimages. 7 – Yoreh, Kametaro, Twocoms. 8 – Abeselom Zerit, Dmytro Pylypenko, GUDKOV ANDREY. 9 – Marc Burleigh. 10 – Netta Arobas, I. Noyan Yilmaz, vladsilver, Tabbiekat. 11 – lazyllama, Marten_House, Anastasiia Tymoshenko. 12 – Tony Campbell, Maksimilian. 13 – Volodymyr Nikitenko, vladimirat, kaschibo, Dennis W Donohue, Volodymyr Burdiak. 14 – SpeedKingz, Dudarev Mikhail. 15 – SpeedKingz, Casimiro PT. 16 – ShutterDivision. 17 – Monkey Business Images, Leonard Zhukovsky, Featureflash Photo Agency, Alastair Wallace, Chones, patat, Mirco Vacca. 18 – Robbi, tanuha2001, chrisdorney. 19 – JT Platt, Rawpixel. com. 20 – miroslav chytil, Amelia Martin, FABRIZIO CONTE. 21 – Amanda Nicholls, mikeledray, Nicole Kwiatkowski. 22 – piotr_pabijan, Elfred Tseng, John Gomez, Frederic Legrand - COMEO. 23 – Ajay K Gopi, Azim Khan Ronnie, Hatchapong Palurtchaivong. 24 – Featureflash Photo Agency, goodmoments. 25 – Jacob_09, Chinnapong. 26 – Monkey Business Images, Jenn Hulls, Anita van den Broek. 27 – FreeProd33, Jesse Davis, Ondrej Schaumann. 28 – Vladimir _Woffka_ Lebedev, Eric Isselee, pixinoo, Noiz Stocker. 29 – FabrikaSimf, Luis Louro, Precisetti79. 30 – . Background on all pages: Flas100. Cardboard & Paper – Andrey_Kuzmin, Palokha Tetiana, NLshop, Picsfive, Andrey Eremin, Adam Cegledi, Flas100. ANATOL, Prostock-studio, Elena Polovinko.
Images are courtesy of Shutterstock.com. With thanks to Getty Images, Thinkstock Photo and iStockphoto.